ALL YOU NEED IS A KETO DIET COOKBOOK

*50 Healthy and Delicious Keto Recipes
for Faster Weight Loss and Metabolism*

Naomie Jones

Table of Contents

Introduction

Keto or ketogenic diet is simply a "low carb diet," with a high fat and protein consumption. Keto diet is often thought to be the same as the Atkin diet. However, they are different. The difference between the two is in the amount of protein consumed.

Another difference is that the keto diet puts the body in ketosis throughout the whole stage. Nevertheless, the Atkin diet only puts the body in ketosis during the first and probably the second phase.

At times, we recommend the ketogenic diet for treating specific ailments. For example, the keto diet can help control diabetes. Also, since the 19th century, the keto diet has been in use for treating epilepsy in children.

One of the gaining use of the keto diet is for weight loss. However, there are other low carb diets that you can use for weight loss. Common examples of such diets are South Beach, Dukan, and Paleo diets. What makes the keto diet stands out is the composition of fat, which is usually between 55-60%.

The word keto is derived from ketosis, which is a natural metabolic process. In other words, we can say that a Ketogenic diet, is that combination of meal which can induce or accelerate the rate of ketosis occurring in the human body. The next argument would be why ketosis is considered healthy? Ketosis is the process in which fats are broken down to release energy and ketones. So, it benefits by producing a good amount of energy, reducing the stored fats from the body and providing ketones for body metabolism. It is noteworthy here that ketosis cannot occur in the presence of freely available glucose or Carbohydrates: in the body. Our usual diet contains more carbohydrates than fats, so naturally, we rely on carbohydrates to extract the required energy. The ketogenic diet is the way of shifting our carb driven body to a fat driven one. To do so, it restricts the daily carb intake to 50grams and recommends a good use of fats instead. All high carbohydrates ingredients are therefore forbidden in this diet plan.

Less sugar intake means lowering the toxic agents in the blood. The same toxins are responsible for causing acne and other skin problems. The ketogenic diet is, therefore, proving to be effective in controlling acne.

When a ketogenic diet was studied to find any prevention or cure for certain types of cancer, the studies suggested that it can indeed be used as a complementary treatment for people who are on chemo and radiotherapy. The ketogenic diet can increase the oxidative stress of the cancerous cells more than the normal cells and hence they can be easily destroyed.

When the ketogenic dieters make health choices and consume, high and good fats contain high-density lipoprotein- HDL. These cholesterols can attach to the bad cholesterol and then removed out of the body. When the cholesterol is no longer deposited in the blood vessel, the heart condition will gradually improve.

This high-fat diet is most effective in boosting brain functioning. As the fats are nourishing for the brain cells and the diet also detoxifies the neurons. This is the reason that a ketogenic diet is highly recommended to people suffering from Alzheimer's, Epilepsy, and memory loss.

There is one added advantage of a ketogenic diet, and that is the people with epilepsy can use to control their seizures. PCOS or Polycystic ovarian syndrome is a medical condition that can bring negative health effects to a woman. And it is a known fact that a high carb diet further aggravates the adverse effects of this condition. Therefore, a ketogenic diet can be used to counter those effects.

The ketogenic diet focuses on reducing your carbohydrate consumption while promoting high fat intake. Protein can be consumed in moderation. The extreme restriction it puts on the carbohydrate consumption may make the ketogenic diet seem like a carb-restrictive diet, but that's not the case. The actual goal of this diet is to encourage a state called "ketosis." Ketosis occurs when the body starts using fats as a primary source of fuel instead of using glucose. Fats are then metabolized for producing ketones. Ketosis happens when your body doesn't have enough glucose.

Glucose is known to create an instant high in the body, followed by a sudden crash. This results in a high level of functioning in the brain, followed by a sudden decline. That's why people who consume high-fat diets experience frequent brain fogs, which hinder their capacity to concentrate on a particular subject. On the other hand, the ketone bodies offer a constant supply of energy without causing any disruption. This is especially beneficial for tissues like the heart and the brain.

Breakfast

Keto Chewy Chaffle

Preparation Time: 5 minutes

Cooking Time: 5 minutes

Servings: 2

Ingredients:

- ½ cup shredded mozzarella cheese, full-fat
- 1 egg, pasteurized
- 2 tsp coconut flour

Directions:

Turn on a mini waffle maker and let it preheat for 5 minutes.

In the meantime, bring out a medium bowl, put all the ingredients in it and then mix by using an immersion blender until smooth.

Ladle the batter evenly into the waffle maker, shut with lid, and let it cook for 3 to 4 minutes until firm and golden brown.

Nutrition:

Calories: 142

Fats: 10g

Protein: 3g

Carbohydrates: 1g

Keto Creamy Bacon Dish

Preparation Time: 5 minutes

Cooking Time: 7 minutes

Servings: 2

Ingredients:

- ½ tsp dried basil
- ½ tsp minced garlic
- ½ tsp tomato paste
- 2 oz. unsalted butter, softened
- 3 slices of bacon, chopped

Directions:

Bring out a skillet pan, put it over medium heat, add 1 tbsp. butter, and when it starts to melts, add chopped bacon and cook for 5 minutes.

Then remove the pan from heat, add remaining butter, along with basil and tomato paste, season with salt and black pepper then stir until well mixed.

Move bacon butter into an airtight container, cover with the lid, and refrigerate for 1 hour until solid.

Nutrition:

Calories: 150

Fats: 16g

Protein: 1g

Carbohydrates: 1g

Eggplant Omelet

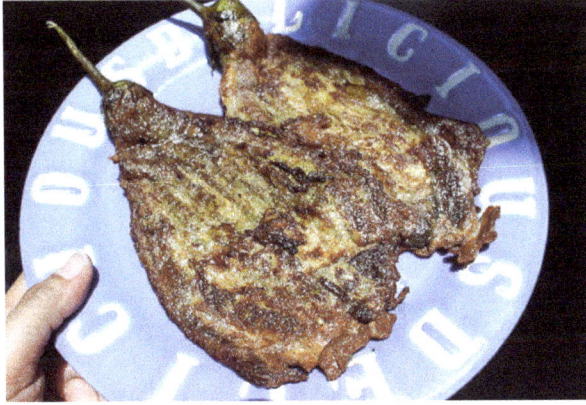

Preparation Time: 5 minutes

Cooking Time: 10 minutes

Servings: 2

Ingredients:

- 1 large eggplant
- 1 tbsp. coconut oil, melted
- 1 tsp unsalted butter
- 2 eggs
- 2 tbsp. chopped green onions

Directions:

Set the grill and let it preheat at the high setting.

In the meantime, prepare the eggplant, for this, cut two slices from eggplant, about 1-inch thick, and reserve the remaining eggplant for later use.

Brush slices of eggplant with oil, spice with salt on both sides, then put the slices on grill and cook for around 3 to 4 minutes per side.

Move grilled eggplant to a cutting board, let it cool for 5 minutes, and then make a home in the center of each slice by using a cookie cutter.

Bring out a frying pan, put it over medium heat, add butter and when it melts, add eggplant slices in it and crack an egg into its each hole.

Allow the eggs cook for 3 to 4 minutes, then carefully flip the eggplant slice and continue cooking for 3 minutes until the egg has thoroughly cooked.

Season egg with salt and black pepper, move them to a plate, then garnish with green onions and serve.

Nutrition:

Calories: 184

Fats: 8g

Protein: 3g

Carbohydrates: 4g

Keto Low Carb Crepe

Preparation Time: 5 minutes

Cooking Time: 8 minutes

Servings: 2

Ingredients:

- 2 eggs
- 1 egg white
- 1 tbsp. unsalted butter
- 1 1/3 tbsp. cream cheese
- 2/3 tbsp. psyllium husk

Directions:

Prepare the batter and for this, put all the ingredients in a bowl, except for butter, and then whisk by using a stick blender until smooth and very liquid.

Bring out a skillet pan, put it over medium heat, add ½ tbsp. butter and when it melts, pour in half of the batter, spread evenly, and cook until the top has firmed.

Carefully flip the crepe, then continue cooking for 2 minutes until cooked and then move it to a plate.

Put the remaining butter then when it melts, cook another crepe in the same manner and then serve.

Nutrition:

Calories: 118

Fats: 7g

Protein: 1g

Carbohydrates: 1g

Keto Cheese Rolls

Preparation Time: 5 minutes

Cooking Time: 0 minutes

Servings: 2

Ingredients:

- 1-oz butter, unsalted
- 2 oz. mozzarella cheese, sliced, full-fat

Directions:

Cut cheese into slices and then cut butter into thin slices.

Top each cheese slice with a slice of butter, roll it and then serve.

Nutrition:

Calories: 166

Fats: 7g

Protein: 2g

Carbohydrates: 0g

Avocado Stuffed with Tuna

Preparation Time: 20 minutes

Cooking Time: 0 minutes

Servings: 2

Ingredients:

- 1 avocado
- 1 can of tuna
- 1 tomato
- ½ onion
- Parsley to taste

Directions:

Cut the avocado into halves. Remove the middle parts so that you can have a room for stuffing. (Keep the "meat" parts)

Cut the tomato and onion into tiny circles.

Mix meat parts with tuna, tomato, and onion.

Stuff the avocado halves with the mixture, decorate with parsley to taste and serve!

Nutrition:

Calories: 132

Fats: 3g

Net Carbs: 6g

Protein: 1.2g

Fiber: 7g

Tuna in Cucumber

Preparation Time: 15 minutes

Cooking Time: 0 minutes

Servings: 6

Ingredients:

- 1 cucumber
- ½ celery leaf
- ½ red bell pepper
- 1 can of tuna
- Pepper and salt to taste

Directions:

Peel the cucumber and cut it into thicker circles. Make a hole in each piece.

Cut the celery and pepper into tiny cubes. Mix them with tuna.

Put 1 tbsp. of tuna mixture into cucumbers.

Add spices to taste and serve.

Enjoy!

Nutrition:

Calories: 109

Total Fats: 1.6g

Net Carbs: 4g

Protein: 1g

Fiber: 5.4g

Small Keto Pies

Preparation Time: 10 minutes

Cooking Time: 30 minutes

Servings: 6

Ingredients:

- 3 eggs
- 5 bacon slices
- ½ red bell pepper
- 1 leek
- ½ cup of broccoli
- 2 oz. of ground cheese
- ½ cup of yogurt
- ¼ pack of baking powder

- 2 tbsp. of olive oil
- Salt, pepper, powdered garlic, parsley to taste

Directions:

Whisk and blend the eggs with baking powder.

Cook the broccoli in water.

Cut bacon, leek and pepper into smaller pieces to taste.

Mix cheese with yogurt well. Then, add bacon, leek, pepper, and spices to taste.

Join the 2 mixtures together and then pour into cupcake or muffin molds.

Bake for 30 minutes at 200°F.

Nutrition:

Calories: 121

Total Fats: 2.1g

Net Carbs: 2g

Protein: 1.3g

Fiber: 6g

Keto Wraps

Preparation Time: 30 minutes

Cooking Time: 0 minutes

Servings: 6

Ingredients:

- 10 oz. of turkey meat
- 3 oz. of bacon
- 1 tomato
- 3 oz. of mozzarella
- Cabbage leaves for wrapping
- For coating:

- 1 cup of mayonnaise
- 6 basil leaves
- 1 tsp. of lemon juice
- 1 tsp. of powdered garlic
- 1 tsp. of salt
- 1 tsp. of pepper

Directions:

Mix all ingredients listed for coating in one bowl. You should get a dense mixture.

Prepare bacon in a frying pan.

Coat cabbage leaves with coating mixture. Pile ingredients over (turkey, tomatoes, bacon and cheese).

Wrap the cabbage like tortillas and serve.

Nutrition:

Calories: 121

Total Fats: 6.9g

Net Carbs: 4g

Protein: 2.4g

Fiber: 5.6g

Chicken Omelet

Preparation Time: 5 minutes

Cooking Time: 10 minutes

Servings: 2

Ingredients:

- 1 oz. of rotisserie chicken, shredded
- 1 tsp. of mustard
- 1 tbsp. of mayonnaise
- 1 tomato, cored and chopped
- 2 bacon slices, cooked and crumbled
- 2 eggs
- 1 small avocado, pitted, peeled and chopped

- Salt and ground black pepper, to taste

Directions:

Heat up a pan over medium heat, grease lightly with cooking oil.

Mix the eggs with some salt and pepper in a bowl and whisk.

Add the eggs in the pan and cook the omelet for 5 minutes.

Add the chicken, avocado, tomato, bacon, mayonnaise and mustard on one half of the omelet.

Fold the omelet, cover pan, cook for 5 minutes and serve.

Nutrition:

Calories: 400

Total Fats: 32g

Net Carbs: 4g

Protein: 25g

Fiber: 6g

Snacks and Sides

Microwave Quick Bread

Preparation Time: 3 minutes

Cooking Time: 2 minutes

Servings: 4

Ingredients:

- 1/3 cup almond flour
- 1/2 teaspoon baking powder
- 1 egg, whisked
- 2.5 Tablespoons ghee or coconut oil, melted

Directions:

Grease a mug then mix all the ingredients in it with a fork.

Microwave for 90 seconds on high

Cool for a some minutes, pop out of mug gently and slice into 4 thin slices.

Nutrition:

Calories: 260

Fat: 26 g

Net Carbohydrates: 2 g

Protein: 6 g

Almond Cheddar Soufflés

Preparation Time: 10 minutes

Cooking Time: 25 minutes

Servings: 8

Ingredients:

- 1 tsp. Dry mustard
- ¾ cup. Heavy cream
- ½ cup. Almond flour
- 6 Large eggs
- Black pepper
- Vegetable oil
- ¼ tsp. Tartar cream

- Salt
- ¼ tsp. Cayenne pepper
- ½ tsp Xanthan gum
- 2 cup. Shredded cheddar cheese
- ¼ cup. Chopped fresh chives
- Cooking spray

Directions:

Whisk together salt, cayenne, almond flour, xanthan gum, pepper, and mustard

Mix in eggs, tartar cream, cheese, chives, and cream as you whisk gently

Set the ramekins with cooking spray then pour in the mixture.

Set your oven for 25 minutes at 350 0F

Enjoy

Nutrition:

Calories: 211

Fat: 17.7g

Fiber: 0.2g

Carbs: 1.4g

Protein: 11.8g

Green Beans & Almonds

Preparation Time: 5 minutes

Cooking Time: 10 minutes

Servings: 4

Ingredients:

- 1 lb. fresh green beans, trimmed
- 2 tbsp. butter
- ¼ cup sliced almonds
- 2 tsp lemon pepper

Directions:

Steam the green beans for 8 minutes until tender, then drain.

On medium heat, melt the butter in a skillet.

Sauté the almonds until browned.

Sprinkle with salt and pepper.

Mix in the green beans.

Nutrition:

Calories: 106

Protein: 3.4 g

Fat: 7.88 g

Carbohydrates: 7.05 g

Sugar Snap Bacon

Preparation Time: 5 minutes

Cooking Time: 5 minutes

Servings: 4

Ingredients:

- 3 cups sugar snap peas
- ½ tbsp. lemon juice
- 2 tbsp. bacon fat
- 2 tsp garlic

- ½ tsp red pepper flakes

Directions:

In a skillet, cook the bacon fat until it begins to smoke.

Put the garlic and cook for 2 minutes.

Add the sugar peas and lemon juice.

Cook for 2-3 minutes.

Remove and sprinkle with red pepper flakes and lemon zest.

Serve!

Nutrition:

Calories: 85

Protein: 5.31 g

Fat: 3.19 g

Carbohydrates: 9.19 g

Flax Cheese Chips

Preparation Time: 10 minutes

Cooking Time: 15 minutes

Servings: 2

Ingredients:

- 1 ½ cup cheddar cheese
- 4 tbsp. ground flaxseed meal
- Seasonings of your choice

Directions:

Set the oven to 425°F.

Spoon 2 tablespoons of cheddar cheese into a mound onto a non-stick pad.

Spread out a pinch of flaxseed on each chip.

Season and bake for 10-15 minutes.

Nutrition:

Calories: 151

Protein: 6.97 g

Fat: 11.72 g

Carbohydrates: 5.95 g

Country Style Chard

Preparation Time: 5 minutes

Cooking Time: 5 minutes

Servings: 2

Ingredients:

- 4 slices bacon, chopped
- 2 tbsp. butter
- 2 tbsp. fresh lemon juice
- ½ tsp garlic paste
- 1 bunch Swiss chard, stems removed, leaves cut into 1-inch pieces

Directions:

On medium heat temperature, cook the bacon in a skillet until the fat begins to brown.

Melt the butter in the skillet then put the lemon juice and garlic paste.

Add the chard leaves and cook until they begin to wilt.

Cover and turn up the heat to high.

Cook for 3 minutes.

Mix well, sprinkle with salt and serve.

Nutrition:

Calories: 359

Protein: 9.93 g

Fat: 35.01 g

Carbohydrates: 1.72g

Baked Tortillas

Preparation Time: 10 minutes

Cooking Time: 30 minutes

Servings: 4

Ingredients:

- 1 large cauliflower, divided into florets.
- 4 large eggs
- 2 garlic cloves (minced)
- 1 ½ tsp herbs (whatever your favorite is - basil, oregano, thyme)
- ½ tsp salt

Directions:

Set the oven to 375°F.

Put parchment paper on two baking sheets.

In a food processor, break down the cauliflower into rice.

Add ¼ cup water and the riced cauliflower to a saucepan.

Cook on medium-high heat until tender for 10 minutes. Drain.

Dry with a clean kitchen towel.

Mix the cauliflower, eggs, garlic, herbs, and salt.

Make 4 thin circles on the parchment paper.

Bake for 20 minutes, until dry.

Nutrition:

Calories: 94

Protein: 5.68 g

Fat: 6.23 g

Carbohydrates: 4.47 g

Asian Style Braised Eggplant

Preparation Time: 15 minutes

Cooking Time: 10 minutes

Servings: 4

Ingredients:

- 2 tsps minced garlic
- ¼ cup coconut milk
- 1 Sliced onion
- 2 tbsps vegetable oil
- 4 chopped green onions
- ½ cup vietnamese sauce
- ½ cup water
- 1 asian eggplant
- 2 tsps chili paste

For the Vietnamese sauce:

- ½ cup chicken stock
- 1 tsp erythritol.
- 2 tbsps fish sauce

Directions:

Set your pan over medium heat then add stock

Mix in fish sauce and erythritol as you sir gently then reserve.

Stir fry the eggplant pieces over medium-high heat until browned evenly then set on a plate.

Again, sauté the onion and garlic on a pan until fragrant.

Add in the eggplant and cook for 2 more minutes

Pour in the water with chili paste, Vietnamese sauce, and coconut milk to cook for 5 minutes as you stir gently.

Top the green onions and cook for another minute.

Enjoy

Nutrition:

Calories: 125

Fat: 10.9g

Fiber: 1.3g

Carbs: 6.4g

Protein: 1.7g

Asparagus Deal

Preparation Time: 13 minutes

Cooking Time: 10 minutes

Servings: 5

Ingredients:

- 40 asparagus spears
- 1/4 cup ghee
- 1 tablespoon lemon juice
- pinch cayenne pepper
- 2 egg yolks
- Salt and black pepper-to taste

Directions:

Take a bowl. Beat the egg yolks very well. Deliver this to a small pan over low heat. Pour lemon juice and whisk well. Combine ghee and whisk until it melts. Add salt, pepper and cayenne pepper. Whisk again well.

Meanwhile; heat up a pan over medium high heat. Put in the asparagus spears and fry them for 5 minutes with tossing.

Divide asparagus on plates. Drizzle the sauce you've made on top.

Serve.

<u>Nutrition :</u>

Calories:150

Fat : 13g

Fiber : 6g

Carbs : 2g

Protein : 3g

Avocado Fries with Almond Mix

<u>Preparation Time:</u> 15 minutes

<u>Cooking Time:</u> 0 minutes

<u>Servings:</u> 3

<u>Ingredients:</u>

- 3 avocados: pitted, peeled, halved and sliced
- 1½ cups almond meal

- A pinch of cayenne pepper
- 1½ cups sunflower oil
- Salt and black pepper to the taste.

Directions:

Mix almond meal with salt, pepper and cayenne in a bowl and stir gently.

Whisk some eggs with a pinch of salt and pepper in another clean bowl.

Cover the avocado pieces in egg and then in almond meal mix.

Add heat to a pan which has oil on medium-high heat source; then add avocado fries and cook them until they show a golden coloration.

Move to paper towels, drain grease and divide into different plates

Serve as a side dish.

Nutrition :

Calories:450

Fat: 43g

Fiber: 4g

Carbs: 7g

Protein: 17g

Fat: 43g

Fiber: 4g

Carbs: 7g

Protein: 17g

Lunch

Crispy Tilapia

Preparation Time: 15 minutes

Cooking Time: 14 minutes

Servings: 4

Ingredients:

- ¾ cup pork rinds, crushed
- 1 packet dry ranch-style dressing mix
- 2½ tablespoons olive oil
- 2 organic eggs
- 4 tilapia fillets

Directions:

Arrange the greased Cook & Crisp Basket in the pot of Ninja Foodi.

Close the Ninja Foodi with crisping lid and select Air Crisp.

Set the temperature to 355 degrees F for 5 minutes.

Press "Start/Stop" to begin preheating.

In a shallow bowl, beat the eggs.

In another bowl, add the pork rinds, ranch dressing, and oil and mix until a crumbly mixture form.

Put the fish fillets into the egg then coat with the pork rind mixture.

After preheating, open the lid.

Arrange the tilapia fillets in the prepared Cook & Crisp Basket in a single layer.

Close the Ninja Foodi with crisping lid and select Air Crisp.

Set the temperature to 350°F for 14 minutes.

Press Start/Stop to begin cooking.

Serve hot.

Nutrition:

Calories: 304

Fats: 16.8g

Carbohydrates 0.4 g

Proteins: 38g

Cod with Tomatoes

Preparation Time: 15 minutes

Cooking Time: 16 minutes

Servings: 4

Ingredients:

- 1-pound cherry tomatoes halved
- 2 tablespoons fresh rosemary, chopped
- 4 cod fillets
- 2 garlic cloves, minced
- 1 tablespoon olive oil
- Salt and ground black pepper

Directions:

At the bottom of a greased a large heatproof bowl, place half of the cherry tomatoes followed by the rosemary.

Arrange cod fillets on top in a single layer, followed by the remaining tomatoes.

Sprinkle with garlic and drizzle with oil.

At the bottom of Ninja Foodie, arrange the bowl.

Close the Ninja Foodi with the pressure lid and place the pressure valve to Seal position.

Select Pressure and set to High for 6 minutes.

Press Start/Stop to begin cooking.

Switch the valve to Vent and do a quick release.

Transfer the fish fillets and tomatoes onto serving plates.

Sprinkle with salt and black pepper and serve.

Nutrition:

Calories: 149

Fats: 5g

Carbohydrates 6 g

Proteins: 21.4g

Crab Casserole

<u>Preparation Time:</u> 10 minutes

<u>Cooking Time:</u> 30 minutes

<u>Servings:</u> 5

<u>Ingredients:</u>

- 2 tbsp. of oil, for frying
- 1 onion, finely chopped
- 150 g finely chopped celery stalks
- salt and pepper
- 300 ml homemade mayonnaise
- 4 eggs
- 450 g canned crab meat
- 325 g grated white cheddar cheese
- 2 tsp. paprika
- ¼ tsp. cayenne pepper

For filing:

- 75 g leafy greens
- 2 tbsp. of olive oil

Directions:

Set the oven to 350°F. Grease a 9x12 baking dish.

Fry onion and celery in oil until translucent.

In another bowl, add mayonnaise, eggs, crab meat, seasonings, and ⅔ chopped cheese. Add the fried onions and celery and stir.

Add the mass to the baking dish. Sprinkle the remaining cheese on top and bake for about 30 minutes or until golden brown.

Serve with salad and olive oil.

Nutrition:

Carbohydrates: 6 g

Fats: 95 g

Proteins: 47 g

Calories: 400

Salmon Skewers in Cured Ham

Preparation Time: 10 minutes

Cooking Time: 15 minutes

Servings: 4

Ingredients:

- Salmon Skewers
- 60 ml finely chopped fresh basil
- 450 g salmon
- salt black pepper
- 100 g dried ham sliced
- 1 tbsp. l Olive oil
- 8 pcs wooden skewers
- Innings
- 225 ml mayonnaise

Directions:

Soak the skewers in water.

Finely chop fresh basil.

Cut salmon fillet into rectangular pieces and fasten on skewers.

Roll each kebab in the basil and pepper.

Cut the cured ham into thin slices and wrap her every kebab.

Lubricate with olive oil and fry on in a pan, grill, or in the oven.

Serve with mayonnaise or salad

Nutrition:

Carbohydrates: 1 g

Fats: 62 g

Proteins: 28 g

Calories: 680

Cheesy Chicken Sun-Dried Tomato Packets

Preparation Time: 15 minutes

Cooking Time: 40 minutes

Servings: 4

Ingredients:

- 1 cup goat cheese
- ½ cup chopped oil-packed sun-dried tomatoes
- 1 teaspoon minced garlic
- ½ teaspoon dried basil
- ½ teaspoon dried oregano
- 4 (4-ounce) boneless chicken breasts
- Sea salt, for seasoning
- Freshly ground black pepper, for seasoning
- 3 tablespoons olive oil

Directions:

Preheat the oven. Set the oven temperature to 375°F.

Prepare the filling. In a medium bowl, put the goat cheese, sun-dried tomatoes, garlic, basil, and oregano then mix until everything is well blended.

Stuff the chicken. Make a horizontal slice in the middle of each chicken breast to make a pocket, making sure not to cut through the sides or ends. Spoon one-quarter of the filling into each breast, folding the skin and chicken meat over the slit to form packets. Secure the packets with a toothpick. Lightly season the breasts with salt and pepper.

Brown the chicken. In a large oven-safe skillet over medium heat, warm the olive oil. Add the breasts and sear them, turning them once, until they are golden, about 8 minutes in total.

Bake the chicken. Bring the skillet into the oven and bake the chicken for 30 minutes or until it's cooked through.

Serve. Remove the toothpicks. Divide the chicken into 4 plates and serve them immediately.

Nutrition:

Calories: 388

Total fat: 29g

Total carbs: 4g

Fiber: 1g

Net carbs: 3g

Protein: 28g

Tuscan Chicken Saute

<u>Preparation Time:</u> 10 minutes

<u>Cooking Time:</u> 35 minutes

<u>Servings:</u> 4

<u>Ingredients:</u>

- 1 pound boneless chicken breasts, each cut into three pieces
- Sea salt, for seasoning
- Freshly ground black pepper, for seasoning
- 3 tablespoons olive oil
- 1 tablespoon minced garlic
- ¾ cup chicken stock

- 1 teaspoon dried oregano
- ½ teaspoon dried basil
- ½ cup heavy (whipping) cream
- ½ cup shredded Asiago cheese
- 1 cup fresh spinach
- ¼ cup sliced Kalamata olives

Directions:

Prepare the chicken. Pat, the chicken, breasts dry and lightly season them with salt and pepper.

Sauté the chicken. In a large skillet over medium-high heat, warm the olive oil. Add the chicken and sauté until it is golden brown and just cooked through, about 15 minutes in total. Transfer the chicken to a plate and set it aside.

Make the sauce. Put the garlic to the skillet, then sauté until it's softened about 2 minutes. Stir in the chicken stock, oregano, and basil, scraping up any browned bits in the skillet. Bring to a boil, then reduce the heat to low and simmer until the sauce is reduced by about one-quarter, about 10 minutes.

Finish the dish. Stir in the cream, Asiago, and simmer, stirring the sauce frequently, until it has thickened about 5 minutes. Put back the chicken to the skillet along with any accumulated juices. Stir in the spinach and olives and simmer until the spinach is wilted about 2 minutes.

Serve. Divide the chicken and sauce between four plates and serve it immediately.

Nutrition:

Calories: 483

Total fat: 38g

Total carbs: 5g

Fiber: 1g

Net carbs: 3g

Protein: 31g

Lamb Leg with Sun-dried Tomato Pesto

<u>Preparation Time:</u> 15 minutes

<u>Cooking Time:</u> 70 minutes

<u>Servings:</u> 8

<u>Ingredients:</u>

For the Pesto:

- 1 cup sun-dried tomatoes packed in oil
- ¼ cup pine nuts
- 2 tablespoons extra-virgin olive oil
- 2 tablespoons chopped fresh basil
- 2 teaspoons minced garlic
- For the Lamb Leg:
- 1 (2-pound) lamb leg
- Sea salt
- Freshly ground black pepper
- 2 tablespoons olive oil

Directions:

To make the Pesto:

Place the sun-dried tomatoes, pine nuts, olive oil, basil, and garlic in a blender or food processor; process until smooth.

Set aside until needed.

To make the Lamb Leg

Preheat the oven to 400°F.

Season the lamb leg all over with salt and pepper.

Bring a large ovenproof skillet over medium-high heat and add the olive oil.

Sear the lamb on all sides until nicely browned, about 6 minutes in total.

Spread the sun-dried tomato pesto all over the lamb and place the lamb on a baking sheet. Roast

Let the lamb rest for 10 minutes before slicing and serving.

Nutrition:

Calories: 352

Fat: 29g

Protein: 17g

Carbs: 5g

Fiber: 2g

Net Carbs: 3g

One-Skillet Green Pasta

Preparation Time: 10 minutes

Cooking Time: 5 minutes

Servings: 4

Ingredients:

- 1 cup shredded mozzarella cheese
- 1 cup grated Pecorino Romano cheese for topping
- 1 egg yolk
- 2 garlic cloves, minced

- 1 lemon, juiced
- 1 cup baby spinach
- ½ cup almond milk
- 1 avocado, pitted and peeled
- 1 tbsp. olive oil
- Salt to taste

Directions:

Microwave mozzarella cheese for 2 minutes.

Take out the bowl and allow cooling for 1 minute. Mix in egg yolk until well-combined.

Lay a parchment paper on a flat surface, pour the cheese mixture on top, and cover it with another parchment paper.

Flatten the dough into 1/8-inch thickness.

Take off the parchment paper and cut the dough into thick fettuccine strands. Place in a bowl and refrigerate overnight.

Place 2 cups water to a boil in a saucepan and add the fettuccine.

Cook for 1 minute and drain; set aside. In a blender, combine garlic, lemon juice, spinach, almond milk, avocado, olive oil, and salt. Process until smooth. Pour fettuccine into a bowl, top with sauce, and mix.

Top with Pecorino Romano cheese and serve.

Nutrition:

Calories: 290

Net Carbs:5g

Fats:19g

Protein:18g

Charred Asparagus with Creamy Sauce

Preparation Time: 5 minutes

Cooking Time: 7 minutes

Servings: 4

Ingredients:

- ½ lb. asparagus, no hard stalks
- Salt and chili pepper to taste
- 4 tbsp. flax seed powder

- ½ cup coconut cream
- 1 cup butter, melted
- ⅓ cup mozzarella, grated
- 2 tbsp. olive oil
- Juice of half lemon

Directions:

Warm olive oil in a saucepan then roast the asparagus until lightly charred.

Season with salt and set aside.

Melt half of butter in a pan and stir until nutty and golden brown.

Add in lemon juice and pour the mixture over the asparagus. In a safe microwave bowl, mix flax seed powder with ½ cup water and let sit for 5 minutes.

Microwave flax egg 1-2 minutes, then pour into a blender.

Add the remaining butter, mozzarella cheese, coconut cream, salt, and chili pepper.

Puree until well combined and smooth. Serve.

Nutrition:

Calories : 442

Net Carbs: 5.4g

Fat: 45g

Protein: 5.9g

Sweet Onion & Goat Cheese Pizza

Preparation Time: 10 minutes

Cooking Time: 40 minutes

Servings: 4

Ingredients:

- 2 cups grated mozzarella
- 2 tbsp. cream cheese, softened
- 2 large eggs, beaten
- ⅓ cup almond flour
- 1 tsp dried Italian seasoning
- 2 tbsps. butter
- 2 red onions, thinly sliced

- 1 cup crumbled goat cheese
- 1 tbsp. almond milk
- 1 cup curly endive, chopped

Directions:

Set the oven to 390°F. Line a round pizza pan using parchment paper. Microwave the mozzarella and cream cheeses for 1 minute. Remove and mix in eggs, almond flour, and Italian seasoning. Spread On the pizza pan, spread the dough then bake for 6 minutes. Melt butter in a skillet, then onions, salt, and pepper and cook on low heat with frequent stirring until caramelized, 15-20 minutes. In a bowl, mix goat cheese with almond milk and spread on the crust. Top with the caramelized onions. Bake for 10 minutes. Scatter curly endive on top, slice, and serve.

Nutrition:

Calories: 317

Net Carbs: 3g

Fats: 20g

Protein: 28g

Dinner

<u>Salmon Rolls</u>

<u>Preparation Time:</u> 15 minutes

<u>Cooking Time:</u> 10 minutes

<u>Servings:</u> 3

<u>Ingredients:</u>

- 1 tbsp. butter
- ½ cup cream cheese
- 1 tbsp. oregano
- 1 tsp cilantro
- 1 tsp salt
- 1 tbsp. dill
- ½ tsp garlic, minced
- 1 oz. walnuts, crushed
- 1 tsp nutmeg
- 10 oz. smoked salmon, sliced

Directions:

In a medium bowl, using a mixer, put butter and cream cheese, then mix until smooth and fluffy.

Add oregano, cilantro, salt, dill, garlic, and walnuts, stir carefully.

Add nutmeg and stir until you get homogenous mass.

Put this cream mixture on each salmon slice and roll them.

Place salmon rolls in the fridge and wait for 10 minutes.

Take out rolls from the fridge and serve.

Nutrition:

Calories: 349

Carbs: 3.98g

Fat: 26.9g

Protein: 23.1g

Cod with Bell Pepper

Preparation Time: 15 minutes

Cooking Time: 1 hour and 30 minutes

Servings: 4

Ingredients:

- 1 bell pepper, seeded and sliced
- ½ small onion, sliced
- 3 garlic cloves, minced
- 1 can sugar-free diced tomatoes
- 1 tablespoon fresh rosemary, chopped
- ¼ cup homemade fish broth
- ¼ teaspoon red pepper flakes
- Salt and ground black pepper
- 1-pound cod fillets

Directions:

In the pot of Ninja Foodi, add all the ingredients except cod and stir to combine.

Season cod fillets with salt and black pepper evenly.

Arrange the cod fillets over broth mixture.

Close the Ninja Foodi with crisping lid and select Slow Cooker.

Set on High for 1½ hours.

Press Start/Stop to begin cooking.

Serve hot.

Nutrition:

Calories: 129

Fats: 1.6g

Carbohydrates: 7.7 g

Proteins: 22.1g

Cheesy Bacon-Wrapped Chicken with Asparagus Spears

Preparation Time: 20 minutes

Cooking Time: 30 minutes

Servings: 4

Ingredients:

- 4 chicken breasts
- 8 bacon slices
- 1 pound (454 g) asparagus spears
- 2 tablespoons fresh lemon juice
- ½ cup Manchego cheese, grated
- From the cupboard
- 4 tablespoons olive oil, divided
- Salt, to taste
- Freshly ground black pepper, to taste

Directions:

Set the oven to 400ºF. Line a baking sheet using parchment paper, then grease with 1 tablespoon olive oil.

Put the chicken breasts in a large bowl, and sprinkle with salt and black pepper. Toss to combine well.

Wrap every chicken breast with 2 slices of bacon. Place the chicken on the baking sheet, then bake in the preheated oven for 25 minutes or until the bacon is crispy.

Preheat the grill to high, then brush with the remaining olive oil.

Place the asparagus spears on the grill grate, and sprinkle with salt. Grill for 5 minutes or until fork-tender. Flip the asparagus frequently during the grilling.

Transfer the bacon-wrapped chicken breasts to four plates, drizzle with lemon juice, and scatter with Manchego cheese. Spread the hot asparagus spears on top to serve.

Nutrition:

Calories: 455

Total fat: 38.1g

Net carbs: 2g

Protein: 26.1g

Bacon-Wrapped Chicken with Cheddar Cheese

Preparation Time: 10 minutes

Cooking Time: 4 hours

Servings: 6

Ingredients:

- 2 large chicken breasts, each cut into 6 pieces
- 6 slices of streaky bacon, each cut in half widthways
- 4 garlic cloves, crushed
- ½ cup Cheddar cheese, grated
- From the cupboard:
- 1 tablespoon olive oil
- Salt, to taste
- Freshly ground black pepper, to taste

Directions:

Grease the insert of the slow cooker with olive oil.

Wrap each piece of chicken breast with each half of the bacon slice, and arrange them in the slow cooker. Sprinkle with garlic, salt, and black pepper.

Put the lid and then cook on LOW for 4 hours.

Set the oven to 350ºF (180ºC).

Transfer the cooked bacon-wrapped chicken to a baking dish, then scatter with cheese.

Cook in the preheated oven for 5 minutes or until the cheese melts.

Take it off from the oven and serve warm.

Nutrition:

Calories: 308

Total fat: 20.8g

Total carbs: 2.9g

Fiber: 0g

Net carbs: 2.9g

Protein: 26.1g

Lamb Burgers with Tzatziki

Preparation Time: 10 minutes

Cooking Time: 20 minutes

Servings: 4

Ingredients:

- 1 lb. of grass-fed lamb
- ¼ cup chives finely chopped green onion or red onion if desired
- 1 tbsp. chopped fresh dill
- ½ tsp dried oregano or about 1 tbsps. freshly chopped
- 1 tbsp. finely chopped fresh mint
- A pinch of chopped red pepper
- Fine-grained sea salt
- 1 tbsp. water
- 2 tsp olive oil to grease the pan

For the tzatziki:

- 1 can coconut milk with all the cooled fat and 1 tbsp. the discarded liquid portion **

- 3 cloves of garlic
- 1 peeled cucumber without seeds, roughly sliced
- 1 tbsp. freshly squeezed lemon juice
- 2 tbsp. chopped fresh dill
- 3/4 tsp fine grain sea salt
- Black pepper to taste

Directions:

To make the tzatziki:

Place the garlic, cucumber, and lemon juice in the food processor and press until finely chopped. Add the coconut cream, dill, salt, and pepper, and mix until well blended.

Put it in a jar with a lid and keep it in the refrigerator until it is served. The flavors become more intense over time when they cool in the fridge.

For burgers:

Thoroughly mix the ground lamb in a bowl with the chives or red onion, dill, oregano, mint, red pepper, and water.

Sprinkle the mixture with fine-grained sea salt and form 4 patties of the same size.

Heat a large cast-iron skillet over medium heat and brush with a small amount of olive oil. Lightly sprinkle the pan with fine-grain sea salt.

Bring the patties into the pan and cook on each side for about 4 min, adjusting the heat to prevent the outside from becoming too brown. Alternatively, you can grill the burgers.

Remove from the pan and cover with tzatziki sauce.

Nutrition:

Calories: 363

Protein: 35.33 g

Fat: 22.14 g

Carbohydrates: 6.83 g

Lamb Sliders

Preparation Time: 5 minutes

Cooking Time: 15 minutes

Servings: 6

Ingredients:

- 1 lb. minced lamb or half veal, half lamb
- ½ sliced onion
- 2 garlic cloves minced
- 1 tbsp. dried dill
- 1 tsp salt
- ½ tsp black pepper

Directions:

Blend the ingredients gently in a large bowl until well combined. Overworking the meat will cause it to be tough.

Form the meat into burgers.

Grill or fry in a pan on medium-high heat until cooked through, 4-5 min per side. If preparing in a pan, to sear both sides quickly, then throw the burgers in a 350° F oven for 10 min to finish cooking through.

Serve with Tzatziki for dipping!

Nutrition:

Calories: 207

Protein: 22.68 g

Fat: 11.89 g

Carbohydrates: 1.17 g

Pasta Orecchiette with Broccoli & Tofu

Preparation Time: 10 minutes

Cooking Time: 15 minutes

Servings: 4

Ingredients:

- 1 (9 oz.) pack orecchiette
- 16 oz. broccoli, roughly chopped
- 2 garlic cloves

- 3 tbsp. olive oil
- 1 tbsp. grated tofu
- Salt and black pepper to taste

Directions:

Place the orecchiette and broccoli in your instant pot. Cover with water and seal the lid. Cook on High Pressure for 10 minutes. Do a quick release.

Drain the broccoli and orecchiette. Set aside. Heat the olive oil on Sauté mode. Stir-fry garlic for 2 minutes. Stir in broccoli, orecchiette, salt, and pepper. Cook for 2 more minutes. Press Cancel and Stir in grated tofu, to serve.

Nutrition:

Calories: 192

Protein: 7.08 g

Fat: 12.6 g

Carbohydrates: 16.93 g

Herbed Portobello Mushrooms

Preparation Time: 10 minutes

Cooking Time: 10 minutes

Servings: 2

Ingredients:

- 2 Portobello mushrooms, stemmed and wiped clean
- 1 tsp minced garlic
- ¼ tsp dried rosemary
- 1 tablespoon balsamic vinegar
- ¼ cup grated provolone cheese
- 4 tablespoons olive oil
- Salt and pepper to taste

Directions:

In an oven, position rack 4-inches away from the top and preheat broiler.

Prepare a baking dish by spraying using cooking spray lightly.

Stemless, place mushroom gill side up.

Mix well garlic, rosemary, balsamic vinegar, and olive oil in a small bowl. Season with salt and pepper to taste.

Drizzle over mushrooms equally.

Marinate for at least 5 minutes before popping into the oven and broiling for 4 minutes per side or until tender.

Once cooked, remove from oven, sprinkle cheese, return to broiler and broil for a minute or two or until cheese melts.

Remove from oven and serve right away.

Nutrition:

Calories: 168

Fat: 5.1g

Carbs: 21.5g

Protein: 8.6g

Garlic 'n Sour Cream Zucchini Bake

<u>Preparation Time:</u> 10 minutes

<u>Cooking Time:</u> 35 minutes

<u>Servings:</u> 3

<u>Ingredients:</u>

- 1 ½ cups zucchini slices
- 5 tablespoons olive oil
- 1 tablespoon minced garlic
- 1/4 cup grated Parmesan cheese
- 1 (8 ounces) package cream cheese, softened
- Salt and pepper to taste

<u>Directions:</u>

Lightly grease a baking sheet using cooking spray.

Place zucchini in a bowl and put in olive oil and garlic.

Place zucchini slices in a single layer in dish.

Bake for 35 minutes at 390oF until crispy.

In a bowl, whisk well, remaining ingredients.

Serve with zucchini

Nutrition:

Calories: 385

Fat: 32.4g

Carbs: 9.5g

Protein: 11.9g

Kale and Lentil Stew

Preparation Time: 10 minutes

Cooking Time: 50 minutes

Servings: 8

Ingredients:

- 5 cups (2 pounds) brown or green dry lentils
- 8 cups vegetable broth or water
- 4 cups kale, stemmed and chopped into 2-inch pieces
- 2 large carrots, diced

- 1 tablespoon smoked paprika
- 2 teaspoons onion powder
- 2 teaspoons garlic powder
- 1 teaspoon red pepper flakes
- 1 teaspoon dried oregano
- 1 teaspoon dried thyme

Directions:

In a large stockpot, combine the lentils, broth, kale, carrots, paprika, onion powder, garlic powder, red pepper flakes, oregano, and thyme. Bring to a boil over medium-high heat.

Cover, reduce the heat to medium-low, and simmer for 45 minutes, stirring every 5 to 10 minutes. Serve warm.

Nutrition:

Calories: 467

Total fat: 3g

Carbohydrates: 78g

Fiber: 31g

Protein: 32g

Desserts

Peanut Butter Fudge Cake

Preparation Time: 10 minutes + 3 hours chilling

Cooking Time: 0 minutes

Servings: 8

Ingredients:

- 3/4 cup peanut butter, sugar-free, preferably homemade
- 3 tablespoons cocoa nibs, unsweetened and melted
- 1/4 teaspoon baking powder
- 3 tablespoons coconut oil, at room temperature
- 1 teaspoon vanilla extract
- 1 stick butter
- 1/3 cup almond milk
- 1/3 cup Swerve
- A pinch of salt
- A pinch of grated nutmeg

<u>Directions:</u>

Melt the butter in your microwave. Stir in the milk, 1/4 cup of Swerve, salt, nutmeg, and baking powder.

Spoon the batter into a parchment-lined baking dish. Refrigerate for about 3 hours or until set.

Meanwhile, make the sauce by whisking the remaining ingredients until everything is well incorporated.

Spoon the sauce over your fudge cake.

<u>Nutrition:</u>

Calories: 180

Fat: 18.3g

Carbs: 4.5g

Protein: 1g

Fiber: 1.1g

Rum Chocolate Pralines

Preparation Time: 10 minutes + chilling time

Cooking Time: 0 minutes

Servings: 8

Ingredients:

- 1 cup bakers' chocolate, sugar-free
- 2 tablespoons dark rum
- 1/8 teaspoon ground cloves
- 1/8 teaspoon cinnamon powder
- 1/2 teaspoon almond extract
- 1/2 teaspoon rum extract
- 3 tablespoons cocoa powder
- 1/4 cup almond butter
- 1 cup almond milk

Directions:

Microwave the chocolate, cocoa, and almond butter until they have completely melted.

Add in the other ingredients and mix to combine well. Pour the mixture into silicone molds and place them in your refrigerator until set.

Nutrition:

Calories: 70

Fat: 3.4g

Carbs: 5.1g

Protein: 2.4g

Fiber: 1.6g

Vanilla Berry Meringues

Preparation Time: 15 minutes

Cooking Time: 1 hour and 45 minutes

Servings: 10

Ingredients:

- 1 teaspoon vanilla extract
- 3 tablespoons freeze-dried mixed berries, crushed

- 3 large egg whites, at room temperature
- 1/3 cup Erythritol
- 1 teaspoon lemon rind

Directions:

In a mixing bowl, stir the egg whites until foamy. Add in vanilla extract, lemon rind, and Erythritol; continue to mix, using an electric mixer until stiff and glossy.

Add the crushed berries and mix again until well combined. Use two teaspoons to spoon the meringue onto parchment-lined cookie sheets.

Bake at 220 degrees F for about 1 hour 45 minutes.

Nutrition:

Calories: 51

Fat: 0g

Carbs: 4g

Protein:12g

Fiber: 0.1g

Hazelnut Cake Squares

Preparation Time: 10 minutes

Cooking Time: 25 minutes

Servings: 8

Ingredients:

- 2 cups almond meal
- 3 eggs
- 1 teaspoon almond extract
- 3/4 cup heavy cream
- A pinch of sea salt
- 1/2 cup coconut oil
- 1/2 cup hazelnuts, chopped
- 3/4 teaspoon baking powder
- 1 cup Erythritol
- 1/2 teaspoon ground cinnamon
- 1/4 teaspoon ground cardamon

Directions:

Set the oven to 365°F. Coat the bottom of your baking pan using parchment paper.

Thoroughly combine the almond meal, baking powder, Erythritol, cinnamon, cardamom, and salt.

After that, stir in the coconut oil, eggs, almond extract, and heavy cream; whisk until everything is well incorporated.

Stir in the chopped hazelnuts. Scrape the batter into the baking pan.

Bake in the oven for at least 25 minutes.

Nutrition:

Calories: 241

Fat: 23.6g

Carbs: 3.7g

Protein: 5.2g

Fiber: 1g

Espresso Pudding Shots

Preparation Time: 10 minutes + chilling time

Cooking Time: 0 minutes

Servings: 6

Ingredients:

- 2 teaspoons butter, softened
- A pinch of grated nutmeg
- 1 teaspoon pure vanilla extract
- 4 ounces coconut oil
- 3 tablespoons powdered Erythritol
- 4 ounces coconut milk creamer
- 1 teaspoon espresso powder

Directions:

Melt the butter and coconut oil in a double boiler over medium-low heat.

Add in the remaining ingredients and stir to combine.

Pour into silicone molds.

Nutrition:

Calories: 218

 Fat: 24.7g

Carbs: 1.1g

Protein: 0.4g

Fiber: 0.7g

Keto Chocolate Nut Clusters

Preparation Time: 5 minutes

Cooking Time: 10 minutes

Servings: 2

Ingredients:

- 9 oz. sugar-free dark chocolate chips
- ¼ cup unrefined coconut oil
- 2 cups salted mixed nuts

Directions:

Line a rimmed baking sheet using parchment paper or a silicone baking mat.

In a microwave-safe bowl, put a piece of the chocolate chips and coconut oil and microwave till the chocolate is melted.

Use a spatula to mix. Let it cool handiest to some degree before using it.

Mix till everything of the nuts is overlaying inside the chocolate.

Drop gigantic spoonfuls of the combo onto the prepared preparing sheet.

Store scraps in the refrigerator for up to three weeks.

Nutrition:

Calories: 170

Fat: 14.9 g

Carbs: 2.9 g

Protein: 3.2 g

Cocoa Coconut Butter Fat Bombs

Preparation Time: 5 minutes

Cooking Time: 10 minutes

Servings: 12

Ingredients:

- 1 cup coconut oil
- ½ cup unsalted butter
- 6 tbsp. unsweetened cocoa powder
- 15 drops liquid stevia
- ½ cup coconut butter

Directions:

In a saucepan, put butter, coconut oil, cocoa powder, and stevia and cook over low heat, frequently stirring until melted.

Melt coconut butter in another saucepan over low heat.

Pour 2 tbsp. of the cocoa mixture into each well of a 12-cup silicone mold.

Add 1 tbsp. of melted coconut butter to each well.

Put in the freezer until hardened, about 30 minutes.

Serve.

Nutrition:

Calories: 297

Fat: 30.6 g

Carbs: 3.6 g

Protein: 1.3 g

Blueberry Lemon Cake

Preparation Time: 10 minutes

Cooking Time: 40 minutes

Servings: 4

Ingredients:

For the Cake:

- 2/3 cup almond flour
- 5 eggs
- ⅓ cup almond milk, unsweetened

- ¼ cup erythritol
- 2 tsp. vanilla extract
- Juice of 2 lemons
- 1 tsp. lemon zest
- ½ tsp. baking soda
- Pinch of salt
- ½ cup fresh blueberries
- 2 tbsp. butter, melted

For the Frosting:

- ½ cup heavy cream
- Juice of 1 lemon
- 1/8 cup erythritol

Directions:

Preheat the oven to 35° F.

In a bowl, add the almond flour, eggs, and almond milk and mix well until smooth.

Add the erythritol, a pinch of salt, baking soda, lemon zest, lemon juice, and vanilla extract. Mix and combine well.

Fold in the blueberries.

Use the butter to grease the springform pans.

Pour the batter into the greased pans.

Put on a baking sheet for even baking.

Put in the oven to bake until cooked through in the middle and slightly brown on the top, about 35 to 40 minutes.

Let cool before removing from the pan.

Mix the erythritol, lemon juice, and heavy cream. Mix well.

Serve.

Nutrition:

Calories: 274

Fat: 23.9 g

Carbs: 8.1 g

Protein: 9 g

Home Made Coconut Ice Cream

Preparation Time: 5 minutes

Cooking Time: 95 minutes

Servings: 4

Ingredients:

- 2 cups evaporated low-fat milk
- ⅓ cup low-fat condensed milk
- 1 cup low-fat coconut milk
- ½ cup stevia/xylitol/yacon syrup
- 2 scoops whey protein concentrate
- 2 tsp. sugar-free coconut extract
- 1 tsp. dried coconut

Directions:

Put all together the ingredients in a mixing bowl and combine well.

Heat the mixture over medium heat until it starts to bubble.

Remove from heat and allow the mixture to cool down.

Chill mixture for about an hour, then freeze in ice cream maker as outlined by the manufacturer's directions.

Nutrition:

Calories: 182

Fat: 1.3 g

Carbs: 18 g

Protein: 22.5 g

Coconut Panna Cotta

Preparation Time: 5 minutes

Cooking Time: 20 minutes

Servings: 2

Ingredients:

- 2 cups skimmed milk
- 1/2 cup water
- 1 tsp. sugar-free coconut extract

- 1 envelope powdered grass-fed – organic gelatin – sugar-free
- 2 scoops whey protein isolate
- 4 tbsp. stevia/xylitol/yacon syrup
- ⅓ cup fresh raspberries
- 2 tbsp. fresh mint

Directions:

In a non-stick pan, milk, stevia, water, and coconut extract.

Bring to a boil.

Slowly add the gelatin and stir well until the mixture starts to thicken.

When ready, divide the mix among small silicon cups.

Refrigerate overnight to relax and hang up.

Remove through the fridge and thoroughly turn each cup over ahead of a serving plate.

Garnish with raspberries and fresh mint, serve and revel in!

Nutrition:

Calories: 130

Fat: 2.5 g

Carbs: 14.4 g

Protein: 29 g

Conclusion

Hopefully, the previous pages can help a beginner feel more comfortable about the keto diet.

It can definitely be overwhelming if a person does not have the necessary information before getting started.

However, once a person has educated themselves, the whole process can seem a breeze.

Knowing the basics of keto, such as how the body reaches ketosis and what that means can be enough motivation on its own for someone to start the diet and stick to it.

The book can help a person move forward from deciding to try to keto to actually making concrete steps in their diet and achieving real results.

Keto can be a great option for people looking to shed extra weight that is stored in their bodies as fat. Ketosis is the process of the body using fats instead of glucose for energy.

The liver can take fats and break them down into ketones, which can be used by both the body and the brain as a fuel source.

To get the body away from using sugars, however, a person has to severely limit the amount and type of carbs they consume so the body can burn through its glucose stores and start working on the fat stores.

This is why it can be so important to stay diligent on the diet once started; otherwise, a person might not see their desired results.

For people who are ready to dedicate themselves 100% to the keto diet, there are various forms of it that can match any person's lifestyle and goals.

The standard keto option is best for people trying the diet for the first time because it can be the quickest way to get into ketosis and reap the immediate benefits.

There are also cyclical and targeted keto for people who might not be willing to follow the strict diet every day. These options give people an opportunity to consume carbs on certain days based on their own personal plans.

Notes:

Lightning Source UK Ltd.
Milton Keynes UK
UKHW020845040621
384922UK00005B/132

9 781801 710527